Intimacy of the Best Kind Is Truly Divine

Rachel L. Fox

Intimacy of the Best Kind Is Truly Divine
Copyright 2015 by Rachel L. Fox

All rights reserved. No part of this book may be reproduced or transmitted in any form or by any means without written permission from the author.

ISBN: 978-1-942013-88-4

Cover design by Pixel Studio
Edited by LACA Bridges
Author photo by George & Ciandra Pitts Photography

Printed in the United States of America by Basar Publishing

Scriptures quoted are from the King James Version, New King James Version, and the Message Bible.

Definitions were taken from Merriam Webster's Dictionary online and dictionary.com

DEDICATION

I give all glory, honor and praise to my Lord and Savior Jesus Christ for giving me the strength and the inspiration to write this book. To my Mom Joyce C. Fox, thank you for walking upright before me - for teaching me what a true virtuous women is. For walking with the Lord and allowing me to see your one-on-one intimate relationship with God even after a divorce- thank you. You chose to live a single life before the Lord. I am eternally grateful for a mom like you; I wouldn't trade you for the world! This book is also dedicated to every single woman out there that has struggled in relationships or has had a hard time with your identity. I pray that this book will bless and change your life. It's time to be happily in love with Jesus!!!

Acknowledgements

I would like to say thank you to all those who made this possible for me. Thank you to Pixle Studios for creating this brilliant book cover. Thank you to George and Ciandra Pitts Photography Dallas, Texas for my author photo. Thank you to LACA Bridges for wonderfully editing my book. Thank you to my "mid-wife" Pastor Rekesha Pitman for helping me birth this baby. Thank you to Basar Publishing for publishing my book. Thanks to Create Space for printing my book and making it easy for Amazon distribution. I would like to thank Mr. Damian R. Bell for giving me the concept for this book. You and your wife, Charlene Bell, have been a blessing to my life- may God continue to bless and keep you. Good deeds never go undone; words of wisdom never go unspoken. I would like to thank Pastor Ramone C. Lynch of Greater Works Church in Newport News, Virginia for writing my letter of recommendation for my author's class so that this process could begin. Thank you for always being there for me and nurturing me over the years like a father would a daughter. Thanks for always having that ear open to listen. You have impacted my life greatly probably more than you even know.

May you and your family be continually blessed. I would like to thank my two big brothers: Minister Daniel L. Fox and Mr. Brian L. Carter. Thank you for the talks of wisdom and thanks for being those male influences in my life. I love you guys so very much. You guys have shown me the good and bad side of dating and I thank you. You both have always been honest with me when it comes to men I have dated in the past. I wouldn't trade you two for the world. Big Brother Daniel, thank you for always leading me down the Godly path. You have always given me the word of God even when I was to stubborn to listen you have been my dad over the years and I have the greatest respect for you always have always will. Thank you to my Best friend of 16 years Natalie Gibbs for just simply believing in me even when I didn't believe in myself. You have always spoken greatness over me you could see what I couldn't see and I love you like a sister. Thank you to Andre and Christine Poole for your words of wisdom and your obedience to God for speaking over my life and helping my transition to Maryland to be smoother. You spoke what thus saith the Lord when everyone else spoke the exact opposite. Thank you for confirming what God spoke to me concerning my life. Lastly, I want to thank my Mentor Eagle Belinda because if you hadn't invited me to T.E.N., I would have never begun this process; I love you for life. This is the beginning of a great book of my life. Thank you for all for your expertise and friendship. May God continue to bless and keep you all.

Table of Contents

Introduction..............................11
Dating Jesus............................15
1 On 1 with You Boo................19
Love Letters to God..................25
Let God be your Man...............32
Falling in love with Jesus............39
Saying I Do.............................46
Sleeping With Jesus..................54
Released to Date Boaz...............61
Definitions of Love....................69
About the Author......................75

Introduction

Have you wondered why all of your past relationships have failed? Have you ever felt like love was not for you or that you would never get married? Well if you haven't, I sure have. I use to think that there was something seriously wrong with me. Over the years, my self-esteem took many hits. I use to think that the men in all of my past relationships didn't love me because I wasn't pretty enough, or maybe my hair was too short or my skin was too dark, or maybe I was just too fat. I use to think I did everything wrong; that's why every man broke up with me. But through all those relationships what God was saying to me was, *Let me love you Boo. If you let me love you, you will choose higher. Those men can only show you the love that they know and only the love that you require. You must know true love to desire true love and to be loved by a man-of-God that can show true love.* God said to me, *Let me take care of you Boo. Let me into those dark places. Let me into those broken places so I can heal you. Get to know me so I can teach you about yourself.* I thought to myself, *Well, well, well, Lord you are on to something here.* God said to me, *Don't think you are not good enough, you are the full package-you just need a little tweaking from me.* He said to me, *I'm going to teach you what to do to correctly prepare for your mate. I have designed a wonderful man for you. But how can you have him if you won't have me? How can you fall in love with him, if you don't first fall in love with me?* I thought to myself, *Wow, Jesus, you dropped a big bomb on me that brought so much clarity and changed my life.* This has been my issue all these years. While I was thinking, my relationship with Jesus was tight, He wanted an even deeper, closer, intimate relationship with Him; I didn't even have a clue.

When I began to understand what God was saying to me, I realized that the relationship I was in had to end. Although I felt like this guy was the first guy I dated that loved me back, I realized that I couldn't love properly and also that his love for me was all he knew and that we would end in destruction. I made a choice, and it was Jesus. This decision was hard for me because all my other relationships ended because they let me go. But all I could think of was: *how can I love properly or be loved properly if I don't first understand how to love and be loved by the Creator of love?* So I said, *Ok God, I'm going to trust you with this one, though difficult and lonely physically.* Spiritually, I had all the company I needed-Jesus was enough. I chose to truly walk this thing out with Jesus.

Choosing to date and fall in love with Jesus is the best decision I could have ever made. I probably would have never learned about myself until marriage, which I'm sure would have taken a turn for the worse. I believe that's why God said, *Let me work on you now and reveal to you my secrets so your future will look much brighter.* I can honestly say, I have never felt better. This has been a journey but well worth it. I cheated on Jesus a few times; I've had many ups and downs, but He helps me get myself back on track. Because He wanted me to share these things with you, this book is a tool to teach and prepare us single women for the right kind of man-of-God. If you never want to get married, you will know how to just commune and have a fun, single life with your God like the Apostle Paul. The single life isn't easily embraced by everyone, but if you can do it, walk it out with the Lord. I pray that everyone reading this book will be truly blessed. It's time to start at the beginning of the map for this journey. The final destination is well worth it. Are you ready? On your mark, get ready, get set, go!!!

Dating Jesus ~
Chapter 1

In a relationship, dating is the process by which you really begin to know one another. This is the part of the relationship where you get to know each other's likes and dislikes. You learn each other's actions and body language. You also really get to get a good understanding of each other. In this process, you figure out if you can live with or live without that person. When it comes to dating Jesus, shockingly, the process is not that much different. You can ask Him questions-He has no problem telling you what He likes and dislikes.

One thing that is a little different is that the Father is not going to lie to you like some of these men do. He is going to tell you the honest truth. Sometimes the truth is not what you want to hear, and it may at times be hurtful. Trust me, it will be what you need to hear and it will be an honest answer.

Another thing that is so unique about dating Jesus is the fact that you will realize that you can't live without Him. When you are in the dating world, many times we get to know a person and realize they are not meant

Intimacy Of The Best Kind Is Truly Divine

for us. When you date Jesus, it's like dating no other guy. He is not a cheap date that you won't call back and won't have a good time with. He is more than fun. He won't ever let you down, and He won't stand you up. He is top notch, and you won't find any one better. His bar is very high.

When I say date Jesus, I mean it in a spiritual and literal way. Go to the movies by yourself and talk to Him there. He will share things with you that you won't believe. I went to see *Act Like a Lady Think Like a Man* by Steve Harvey (this was my first time going to the movies by myself).

While watching this movie, Holy Spirit began to speak to me about real, true love and the dating process- courtship the way He designed it to be. He revealed to me what He expects of me. He also began to tell me things about love and dating that were so wrong in this movie according to the Word of God. When I say I was on a date with Jesus, it was almost as if He were literally sitting in the chair next to me. It was a great experience! Go out to eat with Jesus, yes go out to eat by yourself and have a conversation with Jesus. He will talk to you about your food. He will tell you what to eat and what not to eat. He will even give you advice about what to order. It is a date you will never forget. I know to many this may seem a little strange, but for me, this was the beginning of a lifelong relationship with my number one Boo, Jesus. Go ahead and go on a date with Jesus!

(Stop here and answer questions in your companion guide)

> Ladies it is implementation time don't just read about it, be about it. Don't just let these words cross your mind but get them in your spirit and practice this everyday. This Relationship with Christ is life long. Intimacy Of The Best Kind Is Truly Devine!

1-on-1 with You Boo ~
Chapter 2

When it comes to spending quality time with Jesus, lots of people think you must be laid out on the floor prostrate speaking in tongues, although good sometimes. Other times, God just wants to love on us and us to love on Him. He wants us just speaking and thinking on the things of Him. I am a person who loves music; it is oh-so-easy to spend time with the Father and get into His presence listening to some anointed, contemporary Gospel or whatever Gospel music you may prefer. The Lord loves for His children to sing to Him. The most amazing thing about this is that you don't have to know how to sing or be a great singer to sing to the Lord. The Lord just says, *Make a joyful*

noise! Psalms 100: 1-5 Make a joyful noise unto the LORD, all ye lands.

[2] Serve the LORD with gladness: come before his presence with singing.

[3] Know ye that the LORD he is God: it is He that hath made us, and not we ourselves; we are His people, and the sheep of His pasture.

⁴ Enter into His gates with thanksgiving, and into His courts with praise: be thankful unto him, and bless his name.

⁵ For the LORD is good; His mercy is everlasting; and His truth endureth to all generations.

This scripture is one of my favorites because God gives us direct instructions on how to enter into His presence. We must learn to be in tune with His voice and also how to wait and listen in His presence. God speaks to us concerning the smallest things. There are times when I am at home in the kitchen cooking and the Holy Spirit gives me instructions and recipes about the food I'm cooking. Trust me, cooking with Jesus is the best. Your food will taste far greater than it ever did before. This is a must try! Jesus loves for us to spend time with Him one-on-one all day long. It's so refreshing to do so. Your day will run so much smoother. When I was child I use to hear my mom say, "Well Lord should I eat this apple or this corn?

Should I drink this soda or this water? I know I don't need the soda but Lord, what do you think?" I use to look at my mom like why are you asking Jesus about what food you should eat, I'm sure He has more intriguing conversations to listen to than this. I was so so wrong. God enjoys when we consult Him for the little things. What's important to you is important to Him. He gets a good laugh out of his children- you are sure to put a smile on his face. This is how you build a relationship with Father God. Begin to ask Him about the small things and wait for a response. His sweet, still, calm voice will speak to you. Yes, my God speaks to us; we simply must open our ears to listen. I really did not understand what my mother was doing until I grew in my relationship with God and the Holy Spirit would talk back. God brought my mom and those times she would talk to the Lord about food back to my remembrance, and I had to repent for judging my mom. Don't judge what you know nothing about.

I had no idea how great of an experience my mom was having, until I experienced God talking to me about food and other small things like what outfit to wear. I now knew what it was to spend one-on-one time with my Boo King Jesus. It's an amazing feeling- quite an unforgettable experience. If you talk to God like this often, you will grow and have lots of fun one-on-one time with your Boo Jesus. Yes

I call Jesus *my Boo* because He is just that. Spending time with the Father is sure to put a smile on His face and yours. Talk to Him anytime; He is always listening. Single ladies, He is a much better listener than a lot of these men out here. Talking to and just spending time with Him will help you avoid all the wrong men and prepares you for the man-of-God He wants to bless you with. Spend one-on-one time with your Boo Jesus until He sends your earthly boo. Get to know the Savior of the world. I guarantee, you won't be sorry!

Intimacy Of The Best Kind Is Truly Divine

(Stop here and answer questions in your companion guide)

> Ladies it is implementation time don't just read about it, be about it. Don't just let these words cross your mind but get them in your spirit and practice this everyday. This Relationship with Christ is life long. Intimacy Of The Best Kind Is Truly Devine!

Love Letters to God ~
Chapter 3

Over the years I've been writing all of these love letters to God. I went through so many relationships looking for love in all the wrong places. Every relationship ended because no one ever cared to love me the way I loved them. I can't help the way God created me to be. When I love, I love hard and it's only meant for a real man-of-God. These *wanna-bees* will never understand the woman God created me to be; that's why none of them are in my life.

But the one thing that I was missing while wanting to love and be loved was learning how to let God love me and shape me and mold me. This process is not an easy one, but God has truly taken me on a journey. I had to experience God on a level that most women don't even understand that they can experience God on. God told me to write this book I was like, *What? A book? You know nobody wants to hear what I have to say. I can sing, yeah, but write? Lord have mercy!* but I said ok. God reminded me of all these poems I had in different notebooks. They are all love letters to

Him. God said women need to experience me this way and then they won't have a problem waiting patiently for the one I have for them.

I didn't date for about 3 years and God did some shaping and molding in that time period. I just started dating and this time around, it was different. I admire a man that talks to God on my behalf- there's nothing like it. Back in the day, it was all thugs that couldn't even get a prayer through. I was praying for them like, *Lord change them to see the good.* God was like, *I see all bad, let him go,* but oh no, not me I see the good in everybody. Boy did I learn things the hard way. But life and experience is the greatest teacher; I wouldn't change it for the world.

As a teenager and young adult in the dating process, I was one to write love letters to the guy I was dating. Sometimes writing was a little easier for me than speaking what I was feeling. I love poetry, so I would write love poems to my boyfriend. I was able to express myself with pen and paper in the most beautiful way. Little did I know that I was preparing myself to write love letters to God. On this walk with God as a single woman, I learned that I could write love letters to God. He loves to hear what you think of Him. He adores your love for Him. In return, God will reveal precious secrets to you about Himself and also things that you don't know about you. Writing love letters to God is refreshing and also very intimate.

Here are a few of my love letters that I have written over the years, I hope they bless a single lady out there. Let God love you first, then He will send you Himself in the flesh. This is how I experienced the love of the Father in words...

INTIMACY

Lord, you wrap me in your arms lying
there I feel no harm. To sleep I go with
peace I know your comfort is never wrong.
You rock me in the cradle of your arms
right close to your heart where it's nice and
warm. In this position I am babe-like: so
happy to go to sleep with you through the
night. You rock all hurt away; you comfort
through the pain. You help keep my dreams
holy and if I were to sleep into eternity to
die, to come be with you, is much gain.
Being in your arms is better than any
earthly man because your love last forever

and you won't break my heart no, no never.
I will rest in your presence any time no
matter the season or the weather. It's the
greatest feeling
in the world when me and you Boo are
together. I'll love you Jesus always and
forever.

HOLY GOD YOU ARE

I honor you,
I worship you,
you're the holy God who reigns.
I love you Lord; you are all I need my
strength from day to day.
In the earth there is none like you no other
can compare,
to your love,
your grace,
your mercy,
that's why I worship you today.
Your countless blessings you see fit to give
me even when I'm not deserving. You pick
me up when I let you down. Even when I
can't swim, you never let me drown. You
are the best friend any girl could ever have.
Through life's journeys, you keep me on
the right path. Though the guy below tries

to throw things my way, you step in every time and say, "It's ok baby girl. Focus, it's me you obey." Obedience is better than sacrifice. In your sacrifice of life, your Father you obeyed. Thank you so much for doing what you do. I love you for that Boo. Because of what you did, I can do what I do and that's live a holy, sanctified life, committed, dedicated, completely to you.

P.S. Jesus, I love you Boo

YOUR PRESENCE

In your presence there's fullness of joy. It started in your mother Mary as a baby boy. You grew up to be a great, great king-*The King* of all kings, far greater than any human being. You live on the inside of me- your presence is for real. It's not phony; it's not fake; it's something I can truly feel. Your presence moves through me like a beam of light. With you on the inside, I will always shine bright. I love the way you make me feel. Honey yes I do. That's why you will always and forever be my Boo.

P.S. Jesus I love you Boo.

YOU'RE MY PEACE

Lord you're the peace that passes understanding. The savior of my heart when it is stranded. You're the healer of my heart when it's hurt by others. You're the restorer of my heart when it's been broken from pain and anguish. Lord you are my number one love; no love is greater than yours. You protect my heart; you're the best love of all even when I'm not deserving. I know sometimes I play you like the guy on the side... I'm so sorry Boo, you're number one not number two. You are the head of my life. I apologize for cheating on you; it's never ever worth-it's never ever worth it. Please help me to be faithful to you. The hurt from guys at times is just unbearable. Why do others hurt me so? Lord, I don't understand. I pour out my heart. I pour out my soul; it's always taken for granted. Lord I want to commit my whole life to you. Please Lord do whatever you have to do to show me a man's love is not what I need. Shape and mold me through this pain- this hurtful pain indeed. I'm frustrated Lord and I know it's my fault. If I must go through this brokenness to give you my whole heart, then I guess me and *old boy* will just have to fall apart. It's you that I want, not the love of someone else. It's you that I need so my broken heart won't have to bleed. Take me back Lord I'll try not to leave again. I love you so, so much; you are my deepest and very best friend. Even though I cheated and left you time and time again, I want you to know I'm turning back to you and my love for you will never end. Thank you so much for putting up with me. Without you, I don't know what I would do. That's why I can truly say you will always be my boo.

P.S. Jesus I Love You Boo

(Stop here and answer questions in your companion guide)

> Ladies it is implementation time don't just read about it, be about it. Don't just let these words cross your mind but get them in your spirit and practice this everyday. This Relationship with Christ is life long. Intimacy Of The Best Kind Is Truly Devine!

Let God Be Your Man ~
Chapter 4

Oftentimes as single woman we pray to God for a man. We have that what about me syndrome. We say, Lord when is it my turn? Am I ever going to get married? I'm so tired of being single. I'm a wonderful, loving, God-fearing woman-any man should love to want to be with me. Well I am here to tell you ladies, while all these questions may be true and how we feel, we are so wrong to ask God these questions if we don't even give HIM the time of day. We must first allow God to be our man before we ever ask these questions. Once you start spending time with Him, He will begin to share bits and pieces of who he has for you. We want someone to have companionship with but won't give God any quality time. We are so wrong ladies! We want that special person that we can pour our heart out to and share our secrets with but we won't give Jesus that same respect and really truly He
deserves so much more. Spending time with God and sharing those intimate things deep within you that you would share with an

earthly man is little for God to handle. God deserves to be that go-to person first before you ever even date the one He has for you. We take all this time getting to know different earthly men but don't invest any time in getting to know our spiritual man. Did you know that God is lonely without you? He longs for you. Yes there are millions of people on this earth, but God values you so much that He longs to hear your voice.

A beautiful young woman I met named Dana dropped a bomb in my spirit one day. She told me God would ask her to sing to Him and she would say, *God, you have a million voice choir all over earth why do you care if little old me sings to you?* She said it's a longing that God has for intimacy with you. He wants to spend time with you. The same way you long for a mate, HE longs to be with you. It's so powerful that God Almighty even cares to want to have this time with just you. We should feel special- but we abuse this attribute of God, and ladies we are wrong. Ladies, let God be your man.

Letting God be your man is simply wonderful. No you can't call Him on the telephone, but you can pray and talk to Him all day long; He is always listening. No you can't text Him, but you can get a journal and write Him love letters. He enjoys knowing what you think of Him. No you can't take pictures with Him with your selfie stick, but you can have visions of your Savior embracing you in His love and smiling at you. This is one way to truly make God smile. God is a loving God, and if you need a hug, He can give you one. He can wrap you up nicely. He can wrap His arms right around you and you will feel amazing. If you ever were down and needed a pick me up, God sure can make you laugh. God tells me things all the time that have me rolling. The joy of the Lord is truly my strength. God has a great sense of humor. God knows who you are as a person, and He knows what you like in the opposite sex.

I love a silly man. I love a man that can keep me laughing; God knows this about me. He won't say things that are inappropriate because that's not His character, but He is hilarious- but you don't have to take my word for it. You must talk to Him for yourself. Allow Jesus to be your man. You don't have to be an apostle, pastor or prophet of the Church for God to speak to you. He wants to be your man at whatever state you are in your life. Yes, God speaks to sinners too. He will come find you and make you His boo and make you new! Having a relationship with God is a lot simpler than people think. You can simply open your mouth and commune with the Father; He wants a relationship with you. I talk to Him all day long. My relationship with Him is constant. Sometimes I truly think he gets a kick out of me because I am truly silly and a little analytical at times. I know He is like, *Girl draw your mind in and understand what I'm saying.* When you allow God to be your man, let it all hang out- talk to Him about everything; He has an ear to listen. He will let you know that the things you deal with are not always easy, but with Him, there is no mountain that you can not climb over.

    I can tell you that God is with me. He is truly my boo thang! There is nothing that any earthly man can do for me in my singleness that God can't do. I'm telling you ladies: let God be your man. Not only is He the best man ever, but also He will never leave you nor forsake you. One more thing I can tell you is that He won't cheat on you. We must make sure we don't cheat on Him. When things begin to go south with your relationship with God, trust me ladies, the issue is you Boo; God will never- I say never leave you.

I have cheated on God so many times for these earthly men, yet I was loyal to them. I was just so wrong. How dare I do this to Jesus -cheat on Him like that? I was so ashamed of myself. I have apologized and repented to the Lord for my actions and at times God was like, *Girl, you are something else. Get your life! When you get it this time, don't leave me. A true repented heart lets go of that thing or issue and returns no more.*

With all of my past mistakes and failures God didn't let me go. He forgave me and became my man again. So I say to all of you fearfully and wonderfully-made ladies, let God truly be your man and let my Jesus truly love you Boo. If you do this, you will have no problem patiently waiting on the man-of-God that He has for you. Let Jesus be Boaz Number One and He will prepare you for Boaz Number Two.

(Stop here and answer questions in your companion guide)

> Ladies it is implementation time don't just read about it, be about it. Don't just let these words cross your mind but get them in your spirit and practice this everyday. This Relationship with Christ is life long. Intimacy Of The Best Kind Is Truly Devine!

Falling In Love With Jesus ~ Chapter 5

Falling in love with Jesus for me was not a simple process. The reason is because I had been battered and broken by so many men that I was treating Jesus like them. I literally use to shun Jesus like He did something wrong. I did not know I was doing this, but He revealed it to me. I was just so messed up I didn't know how to love properly. Every time I would get hurt by a man God would say, *let me love you.* I would be like, *I know you love me, but you can't love me like that Lord; that's a different type of love.* Then God would say, *but I love you so much.* I would say, *I know you love me Lord; I love you too.* He was crying out for me to feel his heart for me, but I wasn't getting it. He said to me many times, *I love you; you are beautiful,* and I would say, *thanks Jesus. I love you too,* but did I really love him? Did I really trust Him with my heart? I know to some this may sound strange, and some of you will know exactly what I mean, but this is how it really was for me. I didn't understand God's love and I truthfully I didn't know how to love him in return. The very God that I was serving, that was loving me, I couldn't even understand His love and I didn't know how to love Him in return. One day a shift took place on the inside of me. I was at my best friend Natalie Gibbs' home in Richmond, Virginia and I had been fasting and praying and just spending time singing, talking to and worshipping the Lord. I was going through some emotional battles and I was fasting and praying for God to break whatever it was. I was so broken I couldn't take it anymore. I didn't want to lose myself; I needed God to help me. At this time of my life, I was still not dating. I didn't date for 3 to 4 years. I chose to try and get to know my God a little better and while I was getting to know Him I was getting to know me. All of a sudden, in the midst of worshipping my God, I began to feel different. I use to always feel lonely and unloved. For my whole life up until this point there was an emptiness on the inside of me that I tried to fill, and on that day, Jesus filled it. I felt the heart of God like never before. It was the greatest feeling ever. On that day I fell in love with Jesus for real. I was 27 years old when this happened and I am only 28 now. It has been one lovely year of loving Jesus. When I was able to really feel God's love, He revealed to me how I shut Him out of this area of me for so long. He said, *you pushed me away the same way you pushed away all of the men that hurt you in your life. You had to forget your attitude-even towards me.* He said to me, *you didn't know it and you weren't trying to do it on purpose...* I apologized to God that day and repented for treating Him so bad like He was one of my ex-boyfriends. He forgave me. I forgave myself, and I fell in love with Jesus. God said to me, *I have been trying to share my heart with you for years. You chose to try to find love in a man but that was not the solution to your problem. You needed me.* God was so right. He would say, *I love you daughter* and I would say *I know you love me Jesus,* but that day I really understood and could feel God's love. This was true love and I felt like I could trust God with everything. With my whole heart I in return truly loved Him. I can truly say that *falling in love with Jesus is the best thing I've ever done.* I tell Him all my secrets. At first I would only talk to Him about good things. I use to be so embarrassed and ashamed to talk to Him about the things on the inside of me. Even though He knew already, I just could not talk to Him about it. I didn't feel comfortable telling him everything. I was the same way with my biological father. This is the reason I wouldn't open up to God: I didn't know how.

After this love encounter, I began to trust and love Him like never before and I just spilled my brain and poured out my heart. I realized that I couldn't carry myself. God has been carrying me for so long. Let me tell you I was and still am a heavy load. I know Jesus must have been thinking, *if she would just let me break down the walls of that heart, she will be better. If she would just let me love her, and if she would just love me, this would change her life.* Falling in love with Jesus has taught me to choose higher when it comes to men. I don't mean financial status while that's all good too. I have learned that if the men I date don't have the heartbeat of God, if they don't have a deep intimate relationship with Him, I don't have the time. They can take their good looks and money and jump in the ocean. Any man without God is just toxic waste! If a man is not walking with and being led by God, I don't want him; I will be single. I need a faith-walking, supernatural- believing, man-of-God. I know that this is what God wants for me.

The love of God is like no other. No man on earth can match His love. Even though

God equips men of God to demonstrate love to their wives like Christ did for the church, my Boo Jesus still can't be matched. I want every woman to experience what I have experienced falling in love with Jesus. You can trust Him not with just some things, but you can trust Him with all things, any and everything.

With Jesus I am walking by faith and not by sight, and I am walking in love. I am so wrapped up in God's love. He doesn't allow anyone to take care of me but Him. God truly is my source, no tainted hands tying up my destiny. When I took a faith move from Richmond, Virginia to Maryland just one year ago. God really showed me how much He loves me: I have never been without a thing. God has taken good care of me, and I thank Him for that. I truly love God, and to love Him is to fully trust Him. Trust Him even when you don't know what the outcome is going to be- that's faith. Trust Him even when you are afraid; He won't let you down. Just trust Him, love Him, give Him your whole heart. He will never leave you nor forsake you.

I'm not going to say that every step will be easy, because every step won't be. One thing I can tell you is that it is worth it. Falling in love with Jesus is the best thing ever. He is not like everyone else-He won't let you down. If you are a single woman like me, you want to experience Him this way before you meet your husband. You will know how to truly love and honor your husband once you have learned to love and honor God. Falling in love with Jesus makes the single life so much easier. Being single is a wonderful gift when you fall in love with Jesus. I truly am in love with Jesus and you should love Him too. All you have to do is grab hold of Him. He will teach you to let go of the bitter parts of you. Falling in love with Jesus will change your life forever, and people will see it. When I had my love encounter with Jesus, one of the church mothers of United Nations International in Richmond, Virginia said to me that *there is something different about you.* This church mother's name is Mother Brown; she is sweet and extremely anointed. She said, *God is changing you on the inside and it's shining through on the outside. You are glowing. She don't stop there allow God to keep doing what He is doing. Let Him continue to shape and mold you.* It's amazing because I had truly fallen in love with Jesus and it was a heart, mind, spirit, soul, body and life-changing experience. I hope your experience with my boo Jesus is life-changing too.

(Stop here and answer questions in your companion guide)

> Ladies it is implementation time don't just read about it, be about it. Don't just let these words cross your mind but get them in your spirit and practice this everyday. This Relationship with Christ is life long. Intimacy Of The Best Kind Is Truly Devine!

Saying I Do ~
Chapter 6

Ladies! Ladies! Ladies! You must say, *I Do* to Jesus before you can ever say, *I Do* to the man-of-God He has prepared for you. Yes, you must be married to Jesus. He is the bridegroom and you are the bride. I'm not talking about literally but spiritually. I am also talking about you committing your life to a great relationship with Jesus Christ. You must let go of your plan and your destiny that you desire and marry into the plan of Jesus Christ concerning your life.

When it comes to giving up your will and what you want, it can be very painful. Often times, it's hard to understand why you have to let things go especially when they appear to be going well. In this case, it's best to obey the Lord because He knows the end result and you never know what's down the road may be a tragedy. One of the hardest things I had to do was let go of my fiancé`. I was engaged to be married to a great guy. He had a few issues just like I did but nothing that couldn't be worked through, so I thought.

We had a great relationship. We never got in many arguments. We prayed and fasted for each other, and to me, we got along pretty good. Then one day, I heard the Lord speak to me and say, *You must let him go. I was like what?!* I said, *God why our relationship is great: we are talking about setting a date for our wedding, and we have been talking about children and the city and state we want to live in. We were talking about serious life choices.* I said, *God this, I can't do.* I cried and cried and cried, but then I just said, *Ok* and I was obedient to the Father and I let this man, my love and future husband, father of my future children go. When you begin to say, *I Do* to Jesus and the destiny He has for your life, you must walk in complete obedience. It's not easy. No, No, No it's not easy, but it's worth it. Let go of your plan and begin the great journey of God's plan. Walk in complete obedience. If God tells you Himself to do something or gives a word of revelation, knowledge and wisdom through his prophets, just listen and do what He says- plain and simple. Don't make the mistake of not listening or even turning back like I did. After I let go of this relationship a year later, I went back, and let me just say that was an eye-opener.

One thing I had to learn was that when God tells you to do something, He means what He says. In returning to this relationship with this man, I realized that things were a little different. I had grown a lot in the Lord, but I was still seeking companionship. God was trying to show me He was my companion until He sends the one for me, but I was not seeing this. My eyes ears and heart were blind. So that's what made me go back to my fiancé. Upon returning, I could tell that his love and zeal for God just drifted away; it was gone completely. This left me to wonder if his love for God, for the true and living God, my savior Jesus Christ, was ever there. He had love for a god but not my God. He began to speak things to me that did not line up with the Word-of-God. I would often show him scriptures to prove that what he was saying to me was incorrect. So even with this big red flag right in front of my face, I kept on dating him for a while. He said to me, *if you leave me this time, don't ever think about coming back.* I didn't want to leave him; I loved him too much. But what I was doing at the time was forfeiting my destiny that God had over my life and I wasn't even realizing it. So many red flags, yet I was still in this relationship. Ladies we see the red flags just listen and LIG (let it go) in Jesus Name! So as I continued in this unequally-yoked relationship, I heard God say, *why did you go back? Let that relationship go. Stop going backwards, you must move forward.* I told God that I can't, I truly don't know how to let him go this time. *If you help me God, I won't return back.* But I have learned to be obedient and when you pray for help, God sends it in the craziest ways.

After praying and crying again about a relationship I had gotten myself into, God answered. My fiancé at the time decided he wanted to have a serious talk with me. I will never, ever forget these words. He said to me, *I love you through all your imperfections, through your ups and through your downs, even the things I don't like about you-I love you through them too.* Everything was true but he said one thing to me that completely opened these pretty brown eyes. He said, *would you still love me, be with me and marry me if I choose not to serve Jesus?* I said,
What!!!!! That's like asking me to sell my soul and marry the devil. Even though I loved this man very much at

that time, I knew my love for God was greater. So I told him, *No*, and our relationship ended. We spoke no more after that. I shared a little of my testimony because all of this could have been avoided if I walked in complete obedience from the beginning. The Lord spoke to me and said, *this relationship looks great, but it will end in divorce. You both have a spouse specifically designed for you. I only want you to be married once,* but when I was walking in my will, I did not see it this way. My eyes were now open, and I began to see things the way God was seeing them and things began to change in my life. I said *I Do* to Jesus-to the destiny and will that He had for me. This courtship is not an easy one, but it is sure worth it. For the first time in my life I knew what it was to have companionship and an intimate relationship with my Boo Jesus. He began to reveal some of his precious secrets to me because He could now

trust me. I am so happy I said, *I Do.* This is the good life; He takes care of me so greatly. I am now dating again almost four years later. This guy I am dating has been a blessing to me. He is obedient to God concerning me. He has actually taught me a thing or two about discipline and obedience to God. When you truly align yourself with God and say, *I Do*, you will see that some of your hearts' desires are what He desires for you. God just has HIS timing, we can't go ahead of God's plan. He has chiseled in stone a detailed and specifically designed plan for your life. Don't take a detour and end up off course, but if you do, reel yourself back in. Stick to the map God has planned for you. Sometimes you won't understand or even have a clue about what God is doing, but don't fear the unknown. Don't try to make decisions for God, just do what He says-as crazy as it may sound. I don't care if He says drop everything and move to another state, which I had to do! Just do what He says, don't think twice. What if Jesus decided to get down off that cross and disobey his Father, we would all still be lost. Walking in oneness with the Father is tough, yes, but worth it and trust me, you won't regret it. I haven't!

Intimacy Of The Best Kind Is Truly Divine

(Stop here and answer questions in your companion guide)

> Ladies it is implementation time don't just read about it, be about it. Don't just let these words cross your mind but get them in your spirit and practice this everyday. This Relationship with Christ is life long. Intimacy Of The Best Kind Is Truly Devine!

Sleeping With Jesus ~ Chapter 7

After you have said, *I do* to Jesus, it's time to soak in His presence and let the Father wrap you in His love. At first, soaking in His presence was strange to me. However, my big sister in the Lord, Shaunic Jones, taught me a lot about being in God's presence: how to really just lay there on the floor or on the bed and just wrap myself in His presence. A few times, I would wake up and see her worshipping. She was at the threshing floor, and I didn't have a clue about what she was doing, but I knew it was God. No one had taught me about just getting before the Lord. I knew how to pray, but I didn't know how to just soak in His presence. Sleeping and resting in His presence is just so peaceful...this is where healing takes place. Allow the Holy Spirit to bandage all the open wounds. When sleeping in God's presence, there are times when He doesn't want us to say a word. He just wants us to sit, sleep, lay or rest in His presence. Let Him speak and caress you. Jesus just wants to hold you sometimes. Yes I said it: Jesus can hold you. He can wrap you in His presence. The Holy Spirit just wants to wrap you up and hold you tight sometimes. He can wrap you in His arms and rock you to sleep like your mother or father did when you were a child. This is intimacy you will never forget.

The Holy Spirit gives great comfort. Live and let Him be your companion. He wants to be your everything. When I say everything, I mean everything. Begin to let Him love on you and you in return love on Him. He is yours and you are His forever. There is nothing like the sweet fragrance of His presence. The Holy Spirit will leave His aroma on you which is far greater than any cologne that could stain your clothing from the hug of a man. The sweet fragrance of the Holy Spirit is far greater than any other. When you are lying down sometimes, allow Him to wrap his arms around you. There is this peace, this calmness that will come over you when the Holy Spirit wraps His arms around you. There were times when I would have restless nights and I felt like I needed a hug. I wanted someone to hold me; I was so lonely. I was longing for a feeling that I thought would come from a man, but the Holy Spirit wanted to hold me. So when I felt this way, I began to pray and talk to the Lord about what I was feeling and how I didn't like this feeling of loneliness. I didn't even know how to ask Him to hold me at the time; I just knew how to pray. God heard me because the next thing I knew, I felt like I was wrapped up like a baby. I was so at peace. The Holy Spirit was holding and caressing my spirit. I had never felt this way before- it was another level in my relationship with the Lord. I was so comfortable wrapped in His presence that I drifted off to sleep. I don't even remember when I closed my eyes but when I woke up the next day, I felt refreshed, renewed, rejuvenated and loved. That feeling of loneliness was gone. I had experienced sleeping with Jesus, and it was great. I felt simply amazing. I knew that my Boo, Jesus was there for me and nothing could ever change that. This was an experience to remember.

When I say that Jesus is my everything, He really, truly is my everything. When I say sleeping with Jesus is not a physical or sexual experience it is spiritual, it is spiritual. Yes you must sit, sleep or rest and be still, but this is a caressing of your spirit and soul. This is an experience far greater than just a normal night's rest or a nap. The comfort of the Holy Spirit passes all understanding. Once you begin to just soak and rest in His presence, you will really understand how great God really is. I'm no doctor to prescribe a medicine, but this is a spiritual dose that will heal all elements... but don't just take my word for it, try HIM for yourself.

Intimacy Of The Best Kind Is Truly Divine

(Stop here and answer questions in your companion guide)

> Ladies it is implementation time don't just read about it, be about it. Don't just let these words cross your mind but get them in your spirit and practice this everyday. This Relationship with Christ is life long. Intimacy Of The Best Kind Is Truly Devine!

Released To Date Boaz ~

Chapter 8

In the Bible, in the book of Ruth there is a man named Boaz. Boaz was a wonderful, financially-stable man-of-God with the heart of God. Boaz was a provider and he handled things in the most honest way possible. Then there was a beautiful widow named Ruth. This woman was very humble. Her mother-in-law wanted Ruth to return to her homeland and love again but she said, *No I'm going to stay with you.* She clung to her mother-in-law and they went back home. She deserved love again, but she was all about loyalty and doing things the correct way. Her mother-in-law steered her in the right direction. Ruth was a virtuous woman who chose to walk with the Lord instead of leaving her mother-in-law and going another way. Because of her loyalty, God blessed her with another husband-a great man of God. Boaz in the book of Ruth is a great model for the type of man that a virtuous woman-of-God should desire: a Godly-man, a provider, a gentlemen, and man after God's own heart.

All of the chapters of this book leading up to this chapter was all about preparing yourself. There is a preparation period that every woman should go through before they even think about dating. Once you have dated Jesus, fallen in love with Jesus, spent time with Jesus and allowed Jesus to be your man, then you now have well-prepared yourself for the world of dating. When we take the right steps before dating, then we are very cautious of the type of men we date; we are drawn towards the type of men that God desires for us to have. Dating and getting to know a man of God is ok once you have gotten to know your God. Dating from here gets a lot easier.

Dating Jesus is dating Boaz Number One and your man of God is Boaz Number Two. Don't jump into dating unprepared. You must truly prepare yourself to date the man of God that God desires for you. God requires a man to love his wife like Christ loved the church and a man should be unto his wife and a woman unto her husband. God also requires us ladies to be virtuous women. Proverbs 31:10-31 in the King James Version (KJV) of the Bible states,

10 Who can find a virtuous woman? For her price is far above rubies. **11** The heart of her husband doth safely trust in her, so that he shall have no need of spoil. **12** She will do him good and not evil all the days of her life. **13** She seeketh wool, and flax, and worketh willingly with her hands. **14** She is like the merchants' ships; she bringeth her food from afar. **15** She riseth also while it is yet night, and giveth meat to her household, and a portion to her maidens. **16** She considereth a field, and buyeth it: with the fruit of her hands she planteth a vineyard. **17** She girdeth her loins with strength, and strengtheneth her arms. **18** She perceiveth that her merchandise is good: her candle goeth not out by night. **19** She layeth her hands to the spindle, and her hands hold the distaff. **20** She stretcheth out her hand to the poor; yea, she reacheth forth her hands to the needy. **21** She is not afraid of the snow for her household: for all her household are clothed with scarlet. **22** She maketh herself coverings of tapestry; her clothing is silk and purple. **23** Her husband is known in the gates, when he sitteth among the elders of the land.²⁴ She maketh fine linen, and selleth it; and delivereth girdles unto the merchant.²⁵ Strength and honour are her clothing; and she shall rejoice in time to come.²⁶ She openeth her mouth with wisdom; and in her tongue is the law of kindness.²⁷ She looketh well to the ways of her household, and eateth not the bread of idleness.

²⁸ Her children arise up, and call her blessed; her husband also, and he praiseth her.²⁹ Many daughters have done virtuously, but thou excellest them all.³⁰ Favour is deceitful, and beauty is vain: but a woman that feareth the LORD, she shall be praised.³¹ Give her of the fruit of her hands; and let her own works praise her in the gates.

Ladies, we must prepare ourselves to be wives in our singleness. It's not enough just to pray and desire a man for a husband. We must be wife material. Yes I said it: we must be wife material. Oftentimes women think they are single because they haven't found the right man, but the truth is we oftentimes are not the right woman. We keep attracting junk because we are full of junk. Yes ladies, we must get our emotional selves together and be that woman-of-God for the type of man of God we desire.

Going through the process of dating Jesus is what shapes, shifts, molds and prepares us for our mate. Jesus should be at the center of everything you do. He never leaves us nor forsakes us He is our guide for everything. Having an intimate relationship with God is a lot simpler than some people think. It's time to get on track so we can experience the great things God has for us. If you have grasped everything in this book and have allowed your heart to love Jesus, then you are now released to date Boaz Number Two. You have shown God that He alone is enough for you and that He is all you need. This is the key to having who He has for you. God is a jealous God. He wants our time first and always. He wants to always know He is your number one love. So now, He will release to you the man-of-God He has for you. It's not about asking God for a mate, it's about asking God for more of HIM. He in return will give you Himself in the flesh. To know God is to value Him and He in return values you and releases Boaz Number Two.

It's just so wonderful to love Jesus. Aren't you glad you decided to make Jesus your Boo? I am so glad I decided to date Boaz Number One; He has truly changed my life and prepared me for Boaz Number Two. Jesus I love you Boo!!! Ladies love him because He loves you too. Remember there is no love like His love, because intimacy of the best kind is truly divine!

Intimacy Of The Best Kind Is Truly Divine

(Stop here and answer questions in your companion guide)

> Ladies it is implementation time don't just read about it, be about it. Don't just let these words cross your mind but get them in your spirit and practice this everyday. This Relationship with Christ is life long. Intimacy Of The Best Kind Is Truly Devine!

Definitions of love ~ Chapter 9

Love is a very special, powerful emotion that is often really not understood. The reason why oftentimes we don't understand love is because we don't understand the different types of love. Everyone is not loved the same or on the same level. When we begin to understand the different meanings of love then we can begin to understand how to love according to the Word-of-God. When love is understood, we can also distinguish the type of love we are being showed and the type of love we are showing. We will also began to understand the Father's love for us and the type of love that God expects us to give. Love is required of us. 1 Corinthians 13:1-13 (The Message) if you don't love, you are nothing. God is a God of Love. When He sacrificed himself on the cross for us, He became the greatest symbol of love. No one can match what Jesus did on the cross or
even come close. This type of love is Agape love.

Agape love- Agape love is sacrificial, unconditional love, the highest, greatest love of all 4 types of love shown in the Bible. Agape love is the type of love Jesus has for the Father and for his children. Jesus expressed and poured out agape love by sacrificing himself on the cross for the sins of the world- what an amazing man!

Philio- is the type of love that means close friendship or brotherly love in Greek. Love one another with brotherly affection outdo one another in showing honor. Romans 12:10 (KJV)

Storge- Storge is family love. The bond among fathers, mothers, brothers, sisters. Examples from the Bible- Noah for his

wife, their sons and daughters-in-law. The love Jacob had for his sons. The love sisters Martha and Mary had for their brother Lazarus. These are just a few examples, but we all can use this type of love with our families.

The last type of love shown in the Bible is Eros.

Eros- Eros is physical, sensual love between husband and wife. This definition is in the Song of Solomon between husband and wife. This type of love is shown in sexual intercourse. According to the Bible, sex is forbidden before marriage, so this type of love should be experienced by married couples only. Lots of us prematurely jump into this step and it oftentimes is hard to deal with, so keep yourselves and save this love for your husband or wife. Sex is used for emotional and spiritual bonding and for reproduction. The Apostle Paul noted that it is wise for people to marry to fill their Godly-desire for this type of love. *Now to the unmarried and the widows I say: it is good for them to stay unmarried as I do. But if they cannot control themselves, they should marry for it is better to marry then to burn with passion.* 1 Corinthians 7:8-9 "(NIV) Eros is a necessary part of a healthy marriage, but if you are not married, it's not safe to engage in this type of love. In the Word-of-God there were many different types of love expressed. God shows Himself to us through His love, He reveals and manifest Himself through His love. God is a God of love. When He sacrificed Himself on the cross, He became the greatest symbol of love. Here are a few scriptures to read to about God's love.

John 3:16- For God so loved the world that he gave his only begotten son, that whosoever believeth in him shall (not perish but) have everlasting life. (KJV)
    Definitions of love

1John 4:8- He that loveth not, knoweth not God for God is love. (KJV)

Romans 5:8-But God commands his love toward us in that while we were yet sinners. Christ died for us. (KJV)

John 14:21- He that hath my commandments and keepeth them, he it is that loveth me: and he that loveth me shall be loved of my father, and I will love him and manifest myself to him.

Luke 10:27- and he answering said, thou shalt love the Lord thy God with all thy heart, and with all thy soul, and with all thy strength, and with all thy mind: and thy neighbor as thyself. And he said unto him, this do and and thou shalt live.

1 John 4:7- Beloved, let us love one another but love is of God and everyone that loveth is born of God, and knoweth God.

John 14:15- If you love me keep my commandments.

(Stop here and answer questions in your companion guide)

> Ladies it is implementation time don't just read about it, be about it. Don't just let these words cross your mind but get them in your spirit and practice this everyday. This Relationship with Christ is life long. Intimacy Of The Best Kind Is Truly Devine!

About the Author

Author Rachel Leanne Fox is a native of Newport News, Virginia. She was born on Febuary 2, 1987 to Pastor Spencer L. Fox Jr. (deceased) and Missionary Joyce C. Fox. She has one biological brother, Minister Daniel L. Fox and one half-brother, Mr. Brian L. Carter.

Fox is a current student at Liberty University pursuing her degree in Early Childhood Education with a minor in Christian Counseling. She recently relocated to Maryland under the leading of Holy Spirit to pursue her God and ordained destiny as an author, anointed singer, song writer, teacher and disciple of Jesus Christ. She is single, saved, and successful. Now the owner of Torn II Perfection, a t-shirt and apparel design company, she is also the CEO of the T-Shirt Therapy Fashion Design Camps for Youth. Additionally, she is a member of The Way Clinic Ministries in Glen Burnie, Maryland under the leadership of Apostle Wayne Howden and Prophet Annie Howden. She is a member of T.E.N. Worldwide-the Eagle Network and also a part of The Eagles International Author's Institute.

Eagle Author Rachel Leanne Fox is the author of Intimacy Of The Best Kind Is Truly Divine and Intimacy Of The Best Kind Is Truly Divine the Companion Guide. She is currently working on Intimacy of the Best Kind is Truly Divine For Him- the male version of the book as well as a CD of anointed songs and a series of children's books all to be released in the near future. This anointed woman of God has a heart for God and has a desire for his children to know just how much her God loves them.

Books written

ISBN: 978-1-942013-88-4

ISBN: 978-1-942013-89-1

www.ingramcontent.com/pod-product-compliance
Lightning Source LLC
Chambersburg PA
CBHW061507040426
42450CB00008B/1507